Mechanic Mike's Machines

Speedsters

A+

Smart Apple Media

Published by Smart Apple Media, an imprint of Black Rabbit Books
P.O. Box 3263, Mankato, Minnesota 56002
www.smartapplemedia.com

Produced by David West Children's Books
6 Princeton Court, 55 Felsham Road, London SW15 1AZ

Designed and illustrated by David West

Cataloging-in-Publication Data is available from the Library of Congress.
ISBN 978-1-62588-059-8

Printed in China
CPSIA compliance information: DWCB15CP
311214

9 8 7 6 5 4 3 2 1

Mechanic Mike says:
This little guy will tell you something more about the machine.

 Find out what type of engine drives the machine.

 Discover something you didn't know.

 Is it fast or slow? Top speeds are provided here.

 How many crew or people does it carry?

 Get your amazing fact here!

Contents

The Torpedo

In 1902 on Staten Island in New York, Walter Baker became the first man to break 100 miles per hour (161 km/h) in a car. His streamlined vehicle, *Torpedo,* was also the first car with seatbelts.

Walter Baker steered the car. Seated behind him, E.E. Denzer controlled the brakes.

The top speed of the *Torpedo* was more than 100 miles per hour (161 km/h).

It had 11 batteries and a 14-horsepower electric motor.

Electric cars held the land-speed record in the late 1890s and early 1900s and were much faster than their gasoline engined competitors.

Did you know that the *Buckeye Bullet* broke the electric-powered land speed record at 307.666 miles per hour (495.140 km/h) in 2010?

Mechanic Mike says:
The streamlined design of the *Torpedo* was far ahead of its time. Most cars were box-shaped. After the crash, Baker made two smaller electric cars called the *Torpedo Kids*.

Munro Special

On August 26, 1967, at the Bonneville Salt Flats in Utah, Burt Munro, a New Zealander, set a world speed record on a modified 1920 Indian motorcycle. This record still stands today.

Munro's record of 183.58 miles per hour (295.45 km/h) is for a motorcycle engine smaller than 1,000 cubic centimeters, or cc (61 cubic inches).

Did you know that Munro was 68 years old and rode a 47-year-old machine when he set his record?

The Munro Special achieved an unofficial speed of over 200 miles per hour (320 km/h).

This speedster had room for one rider.

Originally it had a 37-cubic-inch (600 cc) gasoline engine. Munro bored it out to a 58-cubic-inch (950 cc) engine.

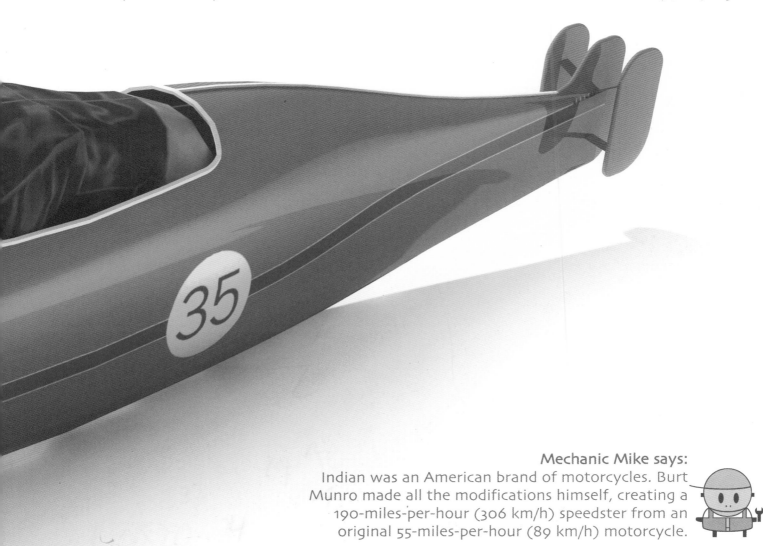

Mechanic Mike says:
Indian was an American brand of motorcycles. Burt Munro made all the modifications himself, creating a 190-miles-per-hour (306 km/h) speedster from an original 55-miles-per-hour (89 km/h) motorcycle.

Mechanic Mike says:
The X-1 was a "bullet with wings." Its shape closely resembled a Browning machine gun bullet, which was known to be stable in **supersonic** flight.

Bell X-1

On October 14, 1947, Captain Chuck Yeager broke the speed of sound in a Bell X-1. This was the first time the sound barrier had been broken by a manned aircraft.

 The X-1 was unflyable at high speed until the British helped by sharing their design for the all-moving tail, which made the aircraft stable.

 Did you know that Chuck Yeager named the aircraft he flew in World War II *Glamorous Glennis* after his wife?

 The X-1 recorded supersonic flight, at **mach** 1.06 (700 miles per hour or 1,100 km/h).

 The Bell X-1 was designed for one pilot.

 The Bell X-1 used a rocket propulsion system.

Hydroplane

These speedsters are a type of boat. They speed along so that very little touches the water. This is called "planing." Hydroplanes are used in racing and in water-speed-record attempts. *Bluebird K7* set seven world water-speed records between 1955 and 1964.

Mechanic Mike says:
Donald Campbell was killed in an accident in the K7 in 1967 while attempting to raise the record to more than 300 miles per hour (480 km/h).

The world water-speed record is held by Ken Warby of Australia and his jet-powered speed boat, *Spirit of Australia*. He reached a speed of 317 miles per hour (511 km/h) on October 8, 1978.

Britain's Donald Campbell designed and drove this *Bluebird K7* hydroplane.

Did you know that Donald Campbell broke several land-speed records as well? All his machines were called *Bluebird*.

The *Bluebird K7* reached a speed of just over 276 miles per hour (444 km/h).

The *Bluebird K7* was **turbojet**-powered.

The X-15 used a rocket engine.

The X-15 had room for one pilot only. Eight of the pilots flew above the height of 50 miles (80 km), so they qualified for astronaut status.

Its maximum speed was 4,520 miles per hour (7,274 km/h).

Like many X-series aircraft, the X-15 was launched from the wing of a B-52 aircraft.

Did you know that two flights by the X-15 went so high, over 62.1 miles (100 km), they qualified as space flights?

Mechanic Mike says:
Twelve test pilots flew the X-15. Among them was Neil Armstrong, who later became the first man to walk on the Moon.

X-15

The X-15 holds the official world record for the highest speed ever reached by a piloted aircraft. It could travel one mile in less than one second and fly to the edge of outer space. X planes were designed to collect valuable data for later spacecraft designs that led to the building of the space shuttle.

13

A jet- and rocket-powered car called *Bloodhound SSC* is being developed to beat 1,000 miles per hour (1,609 km/h).

 Thrust SSC achieved 763 miles per hour (1,228 km/h) for the flying mile.

 The car was driven by Royal Air Force fighter pilot Andy Green.

 Did you know that the date of Andy Green's record came exactly a half-century and one day after Chuck Yeager broke the sound barrier?

 Thrust SSC was powered by two turbofan engines, as used in the British version of the F-4 Phantom II jet fighter.

Mechanic Mike says:
The two turbofan engines used
by *Thrust SSC* burned around 4.8
gallons (18 liters) of fuel per second.

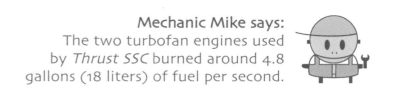

Thrust SSC

On October 15, 1997, this British
jet-propelled car broke the world land-
speed record and became the first car
to officially break the sound barrier.
The runs took place in the Black Rock
Desert in Nevada.

Sailrocket

Sailrocket was built to capture the sailing speed record. On November 24, 2012, Paul Larson used *Sailrocket* to break the record over a distance of 0.3 miles (500 m) and 1 mile (1.6 km).

Mechanic Mike says:
Sailrocket has a wing-shaped sail called an aerofoil. If it was dropped from a great height it would glide down rather than fall.

During an early attempt to break the world record, *Sailrocket* actually took off, flipped over, and cartwheeled before crash-landing upside down. The pilot was not hurt.

Did you know that *Sailrocket* is painted orange in homage to Chuck Yeager's Bell X-1?

Sailrocket reached a top speed of 78.26 miles per hour (125.94 km/h).

Sailrocket has a crew of one, but there is a second cockpit for a passenger.

Sailrocket has no engine. It is powered by the wind.

17

Supercar

Supercars are the fastest and most expensive road cars. They are sleek and eye-catching, and they drive like a race car.

The Hennessey Venom GT has a 427-cubic-inch (7.0-liter) **turbocharged,** gasoline engine.

Like most supercars it has room for a driver and one passenger.

This Hennessey Venom GT has a top speed of 270 miles per hour (435 km/h).

Did you know that it only takes two and a half seconds for the Hennessey Venom GT to reach 60 miles per hour (97 km/h)?

The Bugatti Veyron Super Sport is the only car with a "W engine"—two V engines side by side.

Mechanic Mike says:
The Venom GT is the fastest supercar in the world and has a price of over $1 million.

19

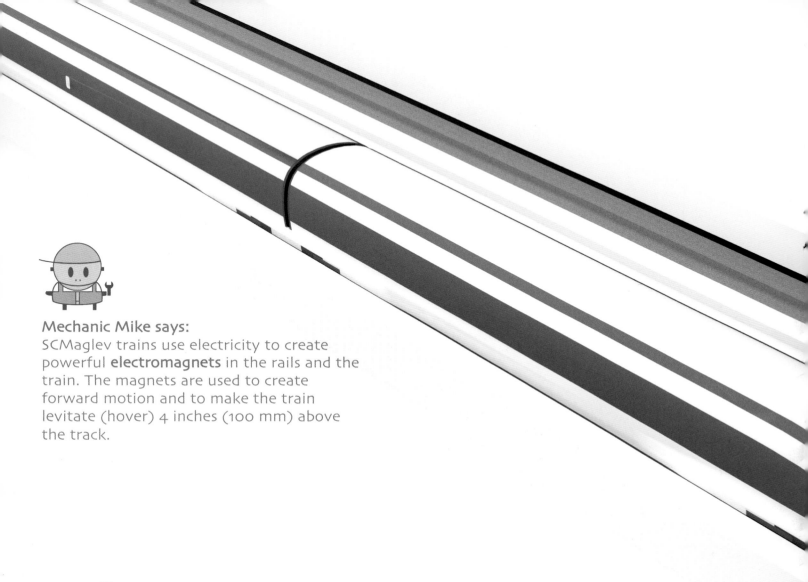

Mechanic Mike says:
SCMaglev trains use electricity to create powerful **electromagnets** in the rails and the train. The magnets are used to create forward motion and to make the train levitate (hover) 4 inches (100 mm) above the track.

SCMaglev trains use superconducting electromagnets powered by electricity.

In 2003, a three-car train reached a speed of 361 miles per hour (581 km/h), a world record for rail vehicles in a manned vehicle run.

These trains are capable of hauling five car sets, each carrying 68 passengers.

Between 1990 and 2008 free rides were given during test runs.

Did you know that the record for the fastest steam train is 126 miles per hour (203 km/h), set in 1938?

20

SCMaglev

The fastest train in the world is the superconducting magnetic levitation train (SCMaglev) in Japan. After testing, SCMaglev trains will go into service, running at 350 miles per hour (500 km/h).

Funny Car

A Funny Car is a type of **dragster** that can cover 1,000 feet (300 m) in only a few seconds. It differs from a dragster by having the engine in front of the driver and a tilt-up, lightweight body shell.

Mechanic Mike says:
The body shell on a Funny Car is an important device. It makes the vehicle more streamlined to punch its way through the air.

Top Fuel dragsters and Funny Cars now run over a 1,000-foot (300-m) distance.

There is only one driver in a Funny Car.

Did you know that funny cars warm up their tires before a race by performing a burnout, which also lays rubber down at the beginning of the track to improve grip?

Cruz Pedregon recorded the quickest run in Funny Car history, covering the 1,000-foot (300-m) distance in 3.959 seconds, at 310 miles per hour (498 km/h).

A funny car's engine is a V8 design with a maximum size of 500 cubic inches (8.19-liter).

23

Glossary

dragster
A long, purpose-built racer with fat rear tires and designed to race over a short straight.

electromagnet
A powerful magnet created by passing electricity through coiled wires.

mach
Unit for the speed of sound.

supersonic
Objects that travel faster than the speed of sound are supersonic.

turbocharged
Extra power gained by a device that uses exhaust gases from the engine.

turbojet
A type of jet engine.

Index